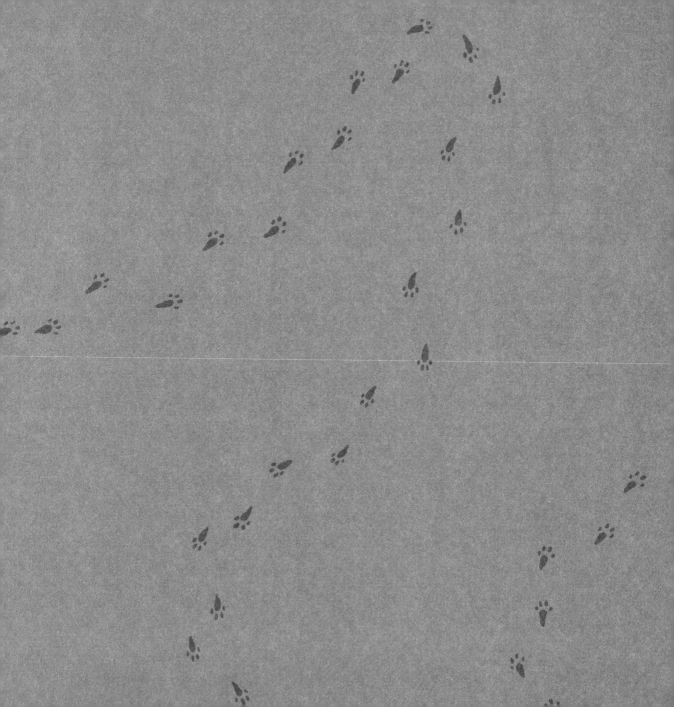

LET'S TALK ABOUT

FEELING AFRAID

by Joy Berry • Illustrated by Maggie Smith

SCHOLASTIC INC.

New York   Toronto   London   Auckland   Sydney
Mexico City   New Delhi   Hong Kong   Buenos Aires

1054261

ISBN 0-439-34149-3

10 9 8 7 6 5 4 3 2 1   01 02 03 04 05

Printed in the U.S.A.
First printing, November 2001

Hello, my name is Squeaky.

I live with Kim.

Sometimes Kim feels afraid.

Sometimes he feels afraid that someone or something is going to hurt him.

Sometimes Kim feels afraid that he might do something that will hurt him.

Sometimes Kim feels afraid when he doesn't know what is going to happen.

When you feel afraid, you feel scared.

Your body might do strange things when you feel afraid.

Your heart might beat faster.

You might breathe harder.

You might perspire more.

Your stomach might feel upset.

Your muscles might feel tense.

You might feel weak.

You might suddenly need to go to the bathroom.

You might feel helpless when you are afraid.

You might feel like running away.

Most of the time you won't like the things that make you feel afraid.

You might not want to be around them.

Feeling afraid isn't good if it keeps you from doing things you need to do.

Feeling afraid is good if it warns you that you are in danger.

Some people pretend they never feel afraid so that others will think they are big and brave.

It's better to admit when you are afraid.

Talk to other people about your feelings.

Ask questions about the things that are scaring you.

Sometimes you'll find out that you don't need to be afraid of what is scaring you.

If you are afraid because you are in danger, try to get away from whatever is scaring you.

If you can't get away from whatever is scaring you, be careful when you are around it.

Avoid doing things that will scare you.

Avoid watching scary movies.

Avoid listening to scary stories.

Avoid thinking scary thoughts that aren't true.

Remember that everyone feels afraid.

Feeling afraid is okay.

The important thing is to do whatever you can to resolve your fear.

Let's talk about... **Joy Berry!**

Joy Berry knows kids. As the inventor of self-help books for kids, she has written over 250 books that teach children about taking responsibility for themselves and their actions. With sales of over 80 million copies, Joy's books have helped millions of parents and their kids.

Through interesting stories that kids can relate to, Joy Berry's *Let's Talk About* books explain how to handle even the toughest situations and emotions. Written in a clear, simple style and illustrated with bright, humorous pictures, the *Let's Talk About* books are fun, informative, and they really work!